MANAGE LIFE

A Treasure of Life's Wisdom from
The Young Prince

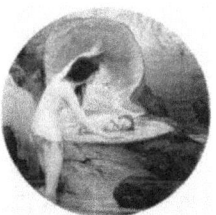

Dr. John Davis Perry II

*F*ar away in The Land of Parables, there is said to have lived a young prince who possessed wisdom that far exceeded his years. This wisdom was granted by the very touch of God per the young prince's request. Understanding the timeless value of the wisdom granted him, the young prince began to entrust to scrolls wondrous wisdom that possessed untold power. After completing his scrolls, the young prince hid them within his treasure of black pearls, calling them his *"pearl of pearls"*. Legend has it, that centuries later, treasure seekers were pillaging for treasure when they happened across the treasure of the black pearls. Some sought to steal the pearls and sell them for fortune. Others took of the profound wisdom, as they sought to gain knowledge and power. It is said, that those who sought for wealth above wisdom, met with mysterious deaths. Those who took of the writings of the young prince, gained wealth beyond their wildest dreams and lived long lives; passing the secrets of the Black Pearls to those found worthy.

~ 2 ~

The Fool of Fools

*There is one who is worse off than the fool -
the wise fool.*

- The Young Prince -

In my own life and in the lives of others, I have noticed a great travesty. The travesty is having great wisdom handed down by God, but not applied to one's personal life. Powerful principles that are not put to practice make the wise, the greatest of fools. At the least, the fool can say "I didn't understand", but what excuse can the wise give?

Do your best not to be a wise fool.

Your Life's Story

When the end comes, and it will, will it be said of me that I was born, I aged, and I died?

-The Young Prince -

I have come to understand that it is not we ourselves that speak of our lives when we meet our end. So, he who is wise writes a little of the story he wants told upon the hearts of men; with his daily actions.

Withering Wisdom

*Is there anyone so wise as to learn by the
experience of others?*

-The Young Prince - (quoting Voltaire)

An unfortunate thing is happening beneath
the sun. Young men reject the wisdom of
the old and pursue wisdom of their own.
However, after their journey has come to an
end, the wisdom they obtained is the same
wisdom in which they rejected. He who is
wise understands that in dying men lies the
treasure of life. Build on the wisdom of
others and you will reach heights beyond
your wildest dreams.

The Two Sides of Love

*Is knowing the depth of love worth knowing
the depth of pain?*

-The Young Prince -

The problem with true love is that it causes
you to give yourself as a gift to another,
despite there being no perfect recipients.
You give yourself over to hands that are
prone to dropping things. If after being
dropped by the one you have given yourself
to, you would rather get over your pain,
push pass your fears and jump back into the
hands that dropped you, it's then helpless,
that you know you have come to know true
love.

The Wounded Smile

A bandage doesn't make a wound disappear.

-The Young Prince -

When you look around, you can see many smiling faces, but there is a smile that serves as a bandage to life's hurts and wounds. Learn to discern the smile of the wounded, because despite the beauty of their smile, when touched, there is yet pain from their unhealed wounds that may cause them to cry and even declare you as their enemy.

The Seeing Blind

The fear of the truth causes the seeing to be blind.

-The Young Prince -

We serve a God of truth, thus we should be people of truth. Never allow your fear of the truth to cause you to accept living in the dark. For the darkness of the unknown is far more fearful than the light of truth. Take courage and choose to see!

The Pleasure of Pain

There is no need to spend life running from pain, because wherever you hide, it will find you.

-The Young Prince -

I've observed many people who have tried to escape the path of pain; not understanding that at the end of its path there awaits a treasure of pleasure. In life, there is pain; and in pain, there is life. It's simply a part of life's process. Learn to process pain instead of mastering avoidance. For the person who can process pain is also the person who can possess a treasure of pleasure.

The Misdirected Fight

Many people are quick to fight others; but, within the darkness of their hearts await the battle of a lifetime.

-The Young Prince -

I've noticed a great evil among our people and that evil is that we are quick to confront others, yet, are unwilling to confront ourselves. Don't waste your time fighting others when there is a personal battle you must fight. For what good is it to win your fight with others, but lose the fight with self.

The Drowning Soul

The drowning soul lives a dreadful death,
daily.

-The Young Prince -

There are many who have yet to learn
how to release disappointment and pain.
As a result, the tears of their inner cries
drown their souls. Attempt to master
rapid release of negative emotions, for
when present too long, they have a
deadly effect on the mind and emotions
of your inner man.

The Day Time Walked Out

Time is like someone who lacks a true heart for you. No matter how much you try to hold on to it, it seeks ways of escape and when gone, thinks very little, if anything more of you.

-The Young Prince -

"Time, oh Time", said the old man, looking with emptiness as he shook his head. "I can recall our moments of laughter, fun and play but those days have passed and you've gone away. Time, I thought we would forever be friends; never would I have thought our friendship would end." Behold, while the old man continued to speak out of his grief, from the distance approached a woman, tall, dark and sleek. "Old man", she replied, 'please do not cry because your old friend Time has left you. I'll stand by your side."

"Come, take my hand. Walk with me, for you and I will begin a new journey." The old man took the mysterious woman's hand, and in his heart of hearts, bade farewell to his old dear friend. As they began their walk, the mystery woman introduced herself: "Old man, I am pleased to make your acquaintance; I am lady death."

Time belongs to no man. What can you do to make the most of your time? For one day, time will surely go its own way.

The Dating Game

Ugliness camouflages itself in beauty.

-The Young Prince -

Ugliness came dressed in garments of beauty on one fair day. All who beheld her were swept away. Win the girl was the desire of every guy, but, little did they know, ugliness was the prize. No matter how beautiful the body, it can't keep hidden the ugliness of the soul.

Discernment of the Heart

Deep within the heart of a man lies the truth; so; master discernment of speech and you will know who's true.

-The Young Prince -

You've heard it said, listen to your heart; but I say, listen to the hearts of others. For the heart is filled with desires and passions that can be heard by the discerning ear. Discern the desire of one's heart through common communication, and after discovering the heart's desire, discern the reason for the desire and you will come to know the intent of another's heart towards you.

Identity

*Are others' many opinions of me a
reflection of the many sides of me?*

-The Young Prince -

Seek to live the kind of life that is so
consistent, that the opinions of men
don't contradict each other. For when
there is no consistency of character,
good deeds are cancelled out by bad,
and one is regarded as a person of no
significance.

~ 16 ~

Man of Honor

*Be a man of honor in a world with no honor,
and you will stand as a great light, in which
all men behold.*

-The Young Prince -

Being honorable will cause you to shine
greater than any achievement; for, even
the wicked achieve things. However,
I've yet to see the wicked achieve being
honorable. The light of honor comes at
great expense, but is well worth the
price; for light in a world of darkness is
priceless.

Many Paths

*In life, we are offered many paths, yet there
is but one way.*

-The Young Prince -

In life we will be offered many
opportunities, but a man of wisdom
sells his soul to purpose and avoids the
pathways of worldly opportunities. For
down them, many have wandered and
have never found their way back home.

Quality of Life

The measure of the quality of one's life is gauged by expectation.

-The Young Prince -

There are three expectations in one's earthly life: the expectation of self, the expectation of others, and the expectation of God. Although all three of these expectations are very much a reality, only one matters in determining the quality of life. Be smart enough not to live life according to others' expectations. Be courageous enough not live life limited by your own expectations. Be strong enough to seek to live your life according to God's expectation; for in doing so, you will have attained a true life of quality.

Right from the Start

You can right a wrong, but the wrong will live on.

-The Young Prince -

In past times, I've done things that have caused pain beyond the moment. And as I attempted to right the wrong, I discovered that it was too late, because pain had enslaved the person I had wronged. Hear wisdom! It is better to do right from the start than to have to right a wrong. For even the most sincere apology doesn't have the power to cause others to forget.

The Simplicity of Greatness

*Selfishness of the human heart has caused
the eyes of humanity to grow dim, the ears
insensitive, and has caused the touch to
become void of compassion. He who learns
to see what others miss, learns to desire
hearing above being heard, and gains a
touch filled with compassion will be
crowned as great among men.*

-The Young Prince -

Those who strive for greatness
oftentimes overlook its simplicity.
Perhaps, that is why those who long to
be great seek to achieve the impossible,
opposed to the possible. Greatness of
character is far more unique than
greatness of accomplishments,
especially in a world driven by
productivity. All that you need for
greatness is within you.

Words of Worth

*Past words are the passwords that help you
pass through the strange and bad lands of
life's experiences.*

-The Young Prince (quoting Ben Zion) -

Many people don't take seriously the things
spoken to them. Words of wisdom are
spoken on today and forgotten by
tomorrow. He who is wise understands that
past words serve as a compass when one
finds themselves in the strange lands of life.
Record worthwhile sayings in your heart
and in a personal book, and the strange
lands of life will not become your home.

The Fact of Fear

Fear makes men believe the worst.

-The Young Prince -
(quoting Quintus Rufus)

Fear has a way of projecting false images that are made alive by internal panic. Some never press beyond their personal panic to facing their fears; thus, they never find their fears to be untruth. Take courage in the face of fear and all will be made clear.

When Evil Triumphs

The only thing necessary for the triumph of evil is for good to do nothing.

-The Young Prince -
(quoting Edmund Burke)

Evil people have given themselves over fully to wickedness; thus, the world is filled with their evil works. The good, on the other hand, are content with trying to keep themselves from doing evil; yet, they do no good. Listen and take this word to heart: *to be good and yet not do good is evil!*

~ 24 ~

Selfish Love

*Although love desires to be loved, it has a
compulsive occupation with giving love.*

-The Young Prince -

One would be wise to fear what we define
as love in our present day society, for true
love does not seek its own best interest.
Remember, the person who is driven by the
desire to be loved rather than the desire to
give love, is a clear example of a
dysfunctional love. They always seek to get
love, but very seldom do they give it. Avoid
them, for they will drain your soul.

Essential Sight

You will never come to know what is essential until you are able to see beyond you.

-The Young Prince -

Each of us must be committed to fighting the darkness that seeks to consume the human heart. For it is a fight in which lies the hope that one's heart will be freed to see beyond the cold, dark prison of self. For the heart that once was imprisoned by self, upon release, can see beyond itself and finally discover that which is truly essential.

Manage Life
Wisdom For Everyday Living

The Young Prince's

Collection of Treasured Quotes

When we remember that we are all mad,
the mysteries disappear and life stands
explained.
-   Mark Twain -

Never argue with an idiot, because they
will drag you down to their level and beat
you with their experience.

In the end, it's not the years in your life
that count - it's the life in your years.
-   Abraham Lincoln -

Life is a process of becoming, a
combination of states we have to go
through. Where people fail is that they
wish to elect a state and remain in it.
This is a kind of death.
-   Anais Nin -

How is one to live a moral and compassionate existence when one is fully aware of the blood, the horror inherent in life, when one finds darkness not only in one's culture but within oneself? If there is a stage at which an individual life becomes truly adult, it must be when one grasps the irony in its unfolding and accepts responsibility for a life lived in the midst of such paradox. One must live in the middle of contradiction, because if all contradiction was eliminated at once, life would collapse. There are simply no answers to some of the great pressing questions. You continue to live them, making your life a worthy expression of leaning into the light.
-    Barry Lopez -

Dost thou love life? Then do not squander time, for that is the stuff from which life is made of.
-    Benjamin Franklin -

If we could see the miracle of a single flower clearly, our whole life would change.
-    Buddha -

There are as many nights as days, and
the one is just as long as the other in the
year's course. Even a happy life cannot
be without a measure of darkness, and
the word "happy" would lose its
meaning if it were not balanced by
sadness.
  -   Carl Jung -

Pain and suffering is inevitable, but
misery is optional.
  -   Unknown -

One cannot become who they need to
be by remaining who they are.
  -   Unknown -

Tragedies sometime happen to allow us
to get rid of things we do not have the
good sense to get rid of by ourselves.
  -   Laurence Cralle Jr. -

Anyone who thinks the sky is the limit,
has a limited imagination.
  -   Unknown -

The best and most beautiful things in the world cannot be seen or even touched. They must be felt with the heart.
-    Helen Keller -

Out of the strain of doing, comes the peace of done.
-    Julia Louise Woodruff -

When your heart speaks, be careful to take good notes.
-    Unknown -

The reason birds can fly and we cannot is because birds have perfect faith; for to have faith is to have wings.
-    J. M. Barrie -

When you were born, you cried and the world smiled. Live your life so that when you die, you can smile and the world will cry.
-    American Indian proverb -

Life is an eternal lesson.
- Unknown -

Learn as much by writing as by reading.
- Lord Acton -

Life can be found only in the present
moment. The past is gone, the future is
not yet here, and if we do not go back to
ourselves in the present moment, we
cannot be in touch with life.
- Thich Nhat Hanh -

It is in our lives and not our words that
our religion must be read.
- Thomas Jefferson -

Life begets life. Energy becomes
energy. It is by spending oneself that
one becomes rich.
- Sarah Bernhardt -

The purpose of life is a life of purpose.
- Robert Byrne -

The person who tries to live alone will
not succeed as a human being. His heart
withers if it does not answer another
heart. His mind shrinks away if he hears
only the echoes of his own thoughts and
finds no other inspiration.
-    Pearl S. Buck -

Happiness is not so much in having as it
is in sharing. We make a living by what
we get, but we make a life by what we
give.
-    Norman Macewan -

There was never yet an uninteresting
life. Such a thing is an impossibility.
Inside of the dullest exterior there is a
drama, a comedy and a tragedy.
-    Mark Twain -

An individual has not started living
until he can rise above the narrow
confines of his individualistic concerns
to the broader concerns of all humanity.
-    Martin Luther King, Jr. -

I've looked at life from both sides now,
from win and lose. Still somehow, its
life's illusions I recall; I really don't
know life at all.
- Joni Mitchell -

What we call the secret of happiness is
no more a secret than our willingness to
choose life.
- Leo Buscaglia -

The irony of man's condition is that the
deepest need is to be free of the anxiety
of death and annihilation; but it is life
itself which awakens it, and so we must
shrink from being fully alive.
- Ernest Becker -

I noticed that nothing I never said ever
did me any harm.
- Calvin Coolidge -

Be glad, for life gives you the chance to
love, to work, to play, and to look up at
the stars.
- Henry Van Dyke -

In the midst of winter, I found there was
within me, an invincible summer.
- Albert Camus -

The universe is infinite in every
direction.
- Freeman Dyson -

You can count how many seeds are in
the apple, but not how many apples are
in the seed.
- Ken Kersey -

Don't cry because it's over;
smile because it happened.
- Unknown -

Little minds are tamed and subdued by
misfortune; great minds rise above
them.
- Washington Irving -

Time is the coin of your life. It is the only coin you have, and only you can determine how it will be spent. Be careful lest you let other people spend it for you.
-    Carl Sandburg -

The real art of conversation is not only to say the right thing at the right place, but to leave unsaid the wrong thing at the tempting moment.
 - Dorothy Nevill -

In life, we shall find many men that are great, and some men that are good, but very few men that are both great and good.
-    Colton -

He is not great who is not greatly good.
-    William Shakespeare -

He is great who is what he is from nature, and who never reminds us of others.
-    Ralph Waldo Emerson -

You will become as small as your
controlling desire; as great as your
dominant aspiration.
- Unknown -

Glory is fleeting, but obscurity is
forever.
- Napoleon Bonaparte -

Even when I am gone, I shall remain in
peoples' minds the star of their rights.
My name will be the war cry of their
efforts, the motto of their hopes.
- Unknown -

About The Author

John Davis Perry II is an author and personal development specialist. He is noted across the country for insightful messages which challenge and inspire his listeners to awaken and actualize the Greater Self.

For over 20 years he has committed himself to the business of helping people through various spiritual and social efforts. In this time Perry developed the personal philosophy, Self-Discovery requires the

willingness to search within. Yet, the actualization of your discovered self, requires the courage to live in harmony with that in which you have become aware." This philosophy he sees as central to manifesting one's Greater-Self, thus it is the underlining framework for his books, CDs. DVD and lectures.

You can receive weekly quotes of inspiration and empowerment by following Perry at:
www.Facebook.com/Johndavisperry
Www.twitter.com/pastorjohnperry

In "What's Stopping Your Shift", Dr. John Davis Perry II, helps you to understand the importance of life's shifts. He also guides you through some personal assessment questions that are sure to show you where you are and the steps you can take toward your next level. Get your copy on Amazon today!

The following websites where used as reference sources for the collection of treasured quotes. All rightful credit has been given to authors of quotation's not written by the author. All efforts have been made to determine authorship of unnamed quotations.

www.wisdomqoutes.com
www.thinkexist.com
www.geocities.com/xanto_pr/Citas.html
www.youquotations.net
www.cyber-nation.com/victory/quotations/subject/quotes_wisdom.html
www.quotegardern.com/philosophy.html
www.heartquotes.net